D1105494

border to border · teen to teen · border to border · teen to teen · border to border

TEENS IN MEXICO

Global connections

BURLINGTON H.S. LIBRARY
BURLINGTON, WI 53105

Teens in Mexico

by Brian Baumgart

Content Adviser: Miguel Angel Centeno, Ph.D.,
Director, Princeton Institute for International and Regional Studies,
Princeton University

Reading Adviser: Peggy Ballard, Ph.D.,
College of Education,
Minnesota State University, Mankato

Compass Point Books  Minneapolis, Minnesota

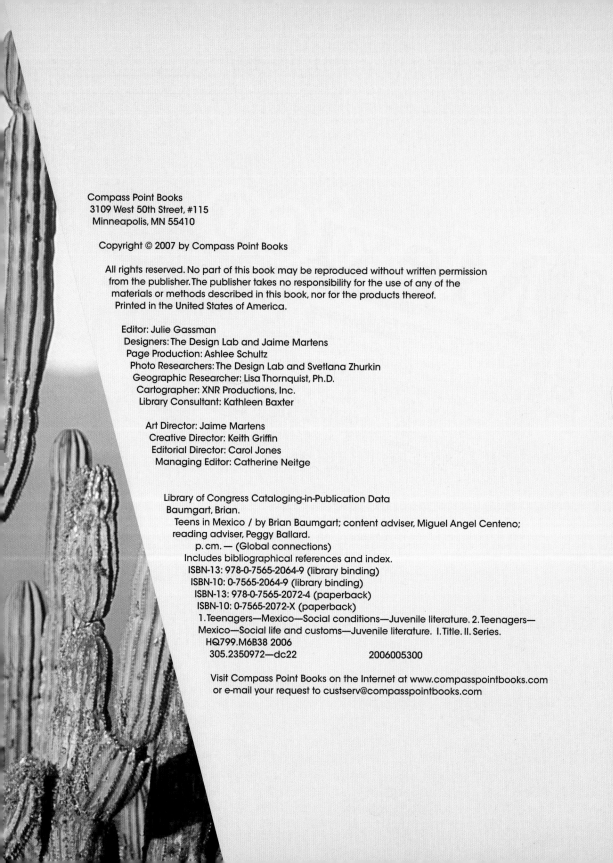

Compass Point Books
3109 West 50th Street, #115
Minneapolis, MN 55410

Copyright © 2007 by Compass Point Books

All rights reserved. No part of this book may be reproduced without written permission
from the publisher. The publisher takes no responsibility for the use of any of the
materials or methods described in this book, nor for the products thereof.
Printed in the United States of America.

Editor: Julie Gassman
Designers: The Design Lab and Jaime Martens
Page Production: Ashlee Schultz
Photo Researchers: The Design Lab and Svetlana Zhurkin
Geographic Researcher: Lisa Thornquist, Ph.D.
Cartographer: XNR Productions, Inc.
Library Consultant: Kathleen Baxter

Art Director: Jaime Martens
Creative Director: Keith Griffin
Editorial Director: Carol Jones
Managing Editor: Catherine Neitge

Library of Congress Cataloging-in-Publication Data
Baumgart, Brian.
Teens in Mexico / by Brian Baumgart; content adviser, Miguel Angel Centeno;
reading adviser, Peggy Ballard.
p. cm. — (Global connections)
Includes bibliographical references and index.
ISBN-13: 978-0-7565-2064-9 (library binding)
ISBN-10: 0-7565-2064-9 (library binding)
ISBN-13: 978-0-7565-2072-4 (paperback)
ISBN-10: 0-7565-2072-X (paperback)
1. Teenagers—Mexico—Social conditions—Juvenile literature. 2. Teenagers—
Mexico—Social life and customs—Juvenile literature. I. Title. II. Series.
HQ799.M6B38 2006
305.2350972—dc22   2006005300

Visit Compass Point Books on the Internet at www.compasspointbooks.com
or e-mail your request to custserv@compasspointbooks.com

Table of Contents

Colorado

Great Lakes

U.S.A.

Ohio

Rio Grande

Mississippi

MEXICO

Gulf of Mexico

THE BAHAMAS

CUBA

BELIZE

GUATEMALA

HAITI

JAMAICA

HONDURAS

DOM. REP.

EL SALVADOR

NICARAGUA

Caribbean Sea

COSTA RICA

PANAMA

Orinoco

VENEZUELA

COLOMBIA

GUYANA

FRENCH GUIANA

SURINAME

ECUADOR

Negro

Amazon

Madeira

PERU

BRAZIL

BOLIVIA

PARAGUAY

CHILE

ATLANTIC

ANDORRA

PORTUGAL
SPAIN

MOROCCO

ALGERIA

TUNISIA

Mediterranean Sea

FRANCE
ITALY
GREECE
ISRAEL
SAUDI ARABIA

Canary Islands

WESTERN SAHARA

MALI

C.A.R.

MAURITANIA

Niger

CONGO

MEXICO
CITY

SENEGAL

GAMBIA

GHANA

TOGO

CAMEROON

CONGO

EQUATORIAL GUINEA

GABON

Congo

IVORY COAST

SAO TOME & PRINCIPE

LIBERIA

ANGOLA

NAMIBIA

7

TEENS IN MEXICO

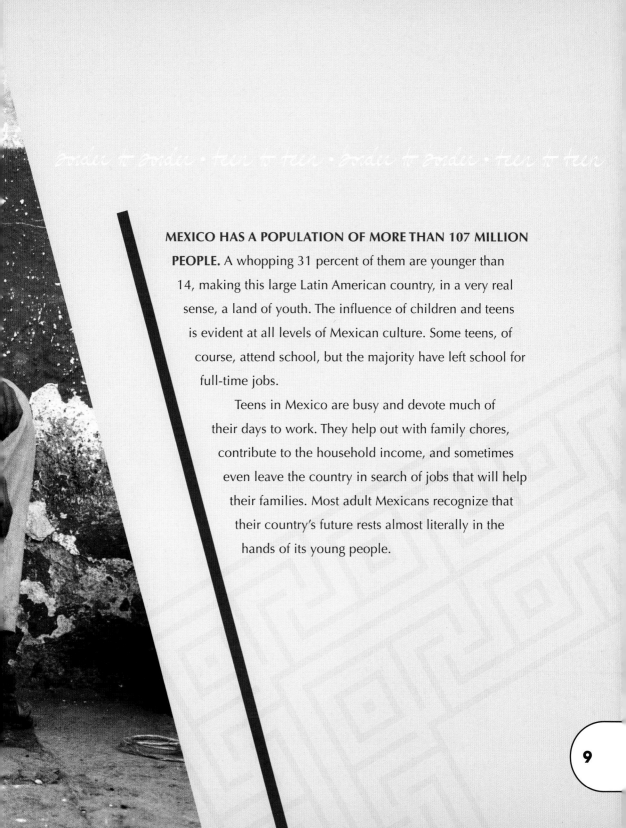

MEXICO HAS A POPULATION OF MORE THAN 107 MILLION PEOPLE. A whopping 31 percent of them are younger than 14, making this large Latin American country, in a very real sense, a land of youth. The influence of children and teens is evident at all levels of Mexican culture. Some teens, of course, attend school, but the majority have left school for full-time jobs.

Teens in Mexico are busy and devote much of their days to work. They help out with family chores, contribute to the household income, and sometimes even leave the country in search of jobs that will help their families. Most adult Mexicans recognize that their country's future rests almost literally in the hands of its young people.

Indigenous students tend to live in rural areas, where walking is the most common way to get to school.

1 Challenges in Education

MEXICAN CLASSROOMS ARE OFTEN CROWDED, WITH NEARLY 50 STUDENTS IN SMALL desks filling the room. They sometimes sit so close to each other that they can hear one another breathing. The uncomfortable conditions, however, do not hinder the desire to learn. The students know the importance of a good education. Since they began mandatory preschool, they've been reminded of this every day by their parents, grandparents, teachers, and clergy.

Mexican government officials have also placed a heavy emphasis on childhood education. Mexican children are required by law to attend preschool classes. In fact, in 2006, Mexico was the only nation in the world in which all children must go to school as early as age 3. After they complete preschool, young Mexicans attend elementary school. Then they move on to three years of secondary, or junior high, school; after that, some of them go still further and attend three years of preparatory, or high, school.

Teen Scenes

It's a little before 2 in the afternoon, and a teen boy is just now settling in at his school desk. In order to accommodate the large student population, his school holds two sessions of classes each day. From 7 A.M. to noon, when the first shift of students are in class, the young man works at his job so he can contribute a little something to his family. But he knows that he needs to keep his grades up. If they suffer, his parents will expect him to quit his job, even though the household needs the extra income he provides.

Meanwhile, another student is opening her books at home. She attended the early school shift. While she doesn't have to head off to a job after school, she does have work to tend to. Both of her parents are employed full time, so she is needed to help care for her younger siblings and the household. But now it's 2 P.M., and she can do some of her homework.

At the same time, a third teen is more than halfway finished with his job for the day. Like the majority of Mexican teens, he has left school for full-time work. His job as an agricultural worker is seasonal. He faces the most important decision of his life—whether he should cross the border into the United States to look for work. His older brother is there, so at least he won't be alone. But he knows the trip is filled with danger.

Most Mexican teens are not able to focus on their studies. The poverty that plagues much of the country makes it necessary for many young Mexicans to earn an income or help their families in other ways.

Grade Levels in Mexican Schools

Level	Grade
Preschool (ages 3–5)	
Elementary School	1–6
Secondary School	7–9
Preparatory School	10–12

Getting to School

The manner in which young people in Mexico get to school each day depends on where they live. Most students who reside in the cities ride either public buses or school-supplied buses, although those who live close to the schools often walk or ride their bikes. In rural areas, walking or bike-riding to school is more common. But rural students who live far from their schools are normally provided with bus or van service.

Public Schools

In addition to requiring all children to attend school, the Mexican government decides what the students in the public schools will study. The official government agency in charge of these schools, the Secretariat of Public Education, sets the general curriculum that must be followed by all of the schools.

As in many countries, the core subjects are reading, writing, and math. Mexican schools also offer courses in science, social studies, and agriculture, as well as physical education, music, and dance. In addition, the public schools in Mexico stress language skills. From primary school through secondary school, students study both Spanish, Mexico's national language, and English. Some Mexican secondary schools also provide courses in German, French, and Italian.

Students who attend private secondary and preparatory schools often continue their educations at private universities.

Private Schools

While Mexico's public schools offer a well-balanced curriculum, they do not offer courses in religion. This is because Mexico's national constitution spells out a strict separation of church and state—and because public schools are state-funded, religious instruction is prohibited in those schools.

As a result, parents who want their children to study religion in school often turn to the country's many private schools. These schools are partly funded by the Roman Catholic Church, Mexico's largest religious organization.

Money to run the private schools also comes from tuition paid by the students' families. As a rule, only teens of middle-class or wealthy families can afford to attend Mexico's private schools.

There is little agreement about which of Mexico's schools are better—public or private. But most people agree on one point: Private schools can often afford to spend more money on each student than public schools can. This allows many private schools to tailor their curricula to fit the specific needs of individual students. As a result, more private school graduates go on to college.

The School Day

The length of the school day varies from place to place and is sometimes determined by the needs of individual communities. Many schools across the country begin classes at 7 A.M. and release students at 2 P.M.

In some Mexican communities, large numbers of students have jobs that require them to work either in the morning or the afternoon. To accommodate these working students, some schools offer a split school day featuring two different shifts. The first shift begins at 7 A.M. and ends at noon; the second shift starts any time after noon and ends around 5 P.M., although it can run into the evening. In such cases, the courses offered and overall quality of education are the same for both shifts.

As a 15-year-old, Jonathan Fonseca Camarena attended public high school in Guadalajara. He started his school day at 2 P.M. and left at 8 P.M. "I like the afternoon shift," he said. "Then I can hang with my friends at night and do my homework in the morning before school."

Another reason schools sometimes offer shifts is to alleviate overcrowding in classrooms.

The skirts of school uniforms are a variety of colors, from navy to plaid to pink.

Whether they attend the first or second shift, and whether they go to a public or private school, most Mexican students have one thing in common. That is, they are required to wear some kind of school uniform. These uniforms vary from community to community and from school to school. In most public schools, the required dress consists of a white blouse and a skirt for girls and a white dress shirt and khaki pants for boys. In contrast, a few public schools and many private schools require a more formal uniform for their students.

School Struggles

Paying for the more formal uniforms can be difficult for some students because of low family incomes. In 2004, about 50 percent of Mexican families lived in poverty. And lack of money, both in families and in the budgets of many communities, is the primary root of a number of other problems that plague both urban and rural schools in Mexico.

Among the most serious of these problems is overcrowding in many classrooms. In the poorest schools, some classrooms contain between 40 and 50 students, who sit at small desks wedged close together. This makes it difficult for teachers to provide individual instruction to those who need it.

Poverty also affects the dropout rate in Mexican schools. Because they need to earn money to help support their families, some young people leave school before graduating to get full-time jobs. For example, more than 300,000 Mexican teens drop out of school each year after completing the sixth grade, the last year of primary school. And more than half of Mexican students leave school by the age of 14.

Still another persistent problem that lack of money has caused in Mexico's educational system is the poor physical condition of some primary and secondary schools. A number of schools, especially those serving low-income neighborhoods and towns, are old and badly in need of repair.

Also, during Mexico's rainy season (lasting from June to October), several

Eight small classrooms without electricity serve 170 students in an elementary school in Chimalhuacan, an area of Mexico City.

Puddle-Free Learning

Belisario Domínguez Palencia, a public school in the flood-prone southeastern coastal state of Tabasco, is one of the schools that has been helped by the Basic Education Development Project. Students used to attend class in *palapas.* These open structures could not protect students from stormy weather—when it rained, the students got wet. But today students attend class in rooms made of concrete. "During the rainy season, water used to come from everywhere," said Jaime Magaña, head of the school. "We would do as the chickens do and huddle close together. Now they have built us four rooms and I don't want to brag, but it is one of the best-equipped schools in the area."

palapas
pa-LAH-pas

schools in the coastal areas suffer flood damage. Money to rebuild these facilities is needed on a fairly regular basis. However, help is on the way. In the early 1990s, a special government initiative called the Basic Education Development Project was created to help repair and rebuild schools. Thanks to this program, the proportion of schools in poor condition dropped from 14 percent in 1991 to 9 percent in 2003.

Not all of the problems in Mexico's schools are the result of a lack of funding. To some degree, cultural differences within the country also make it difficult for schools to teach and for children to learn. For instance, several of Mexico's southern and coastal states, such as Chiapas, Guerrero, and Oaxaca, have populations with a higher-than-average proportion of indigenous people. The indigenous groups are mostly the descendants of Indian tribes that inhabited the area when the Spanish arrived in the 1500s.

Today indigenous people make up about 13 percent of the population. As many as 60 native languages are spoken among these people, many of whom speak little or no Spanish. Teaching millions to speak the national language obviously presents a major challenge for the government. One factor making that challenge so difficult is that it is often hard to find teachers who are fluent in both Spanish and one or more native languages.

Students in El Provenir, Chiapas, have benefited from an aid program that allows the community to purchase computers. A wealthy municipality, Pedro Garza Garcia, provides funding to the community.

Telesecundarias

telesecundarias
tay-lay-say-coon-DA-ree-ahs

Because of the difficulty of getting high-quality education in many rural areas of Mexico, the country has established a system of satellite distance-learning courses for secondary education. The schools that use this system are called *telesecundarias*. They allow students in small towns and rural communities to watch televised lectures and prerecorded educational science programs that are transmitted by satellite. This satellite system is called EduSat. By 2005, this program had connected 30,000 schools, 300,000 teachers, and more than 3 million students throughout the country.

City plazas provide urban teens with a place to sit and talk.

CHAPTER TWO

Lifestyles in Contrast

MEXICO IS NOT ONLY A LAND OF YOUTH, IT IS ALSO A COUNTRY DOMINATED IN MANY WAYS BY CITIES AND CITY LIFE. There are nine cities in Mexico with populations of a million people or more, among them Mexico City, Guadalajara, Puebla, and Tijuana. The country also has 16 additional cities with populations in excess of half a million people. In fact, Mexico is so highly urbanized that at least 70 percent of the country's people live in cities.

There the pace of life is fast. City-dwelling teens have access to some of the advantages of urban life, such as public transportation, theaters, museums, and a wide array of restaurants. But they also must deal with the disadvantages of urban life—especially overcrowding, noise, and smog.

Mexico City covers more than 800 square miles (2,000 square kilometers).

In the rural portions of Mexico, by contrast, the pace of life for teens is more leisurely. The countryside is quieter and far less populated than the cities. Most of the food consumed in the cities is grown on rural farms. This means that the city dwellers depend on the countryside for food, while the rural folk depend in large degree on the money they make selling that food. Therefore, though life is quite different in each area, Mexico's urban and rural regions are interdependent.

Life in the Cities

Throughout the 20th century, Mexico's cities experienced rapid population growth. The most noticeable example was the nation's capital, Mexico City, which witnessed nothing less than spectacular growth. In 1950, the city had about 3 million inhabitants; by 2000, that number had risen to 18 million. In 2006, Mexico City supported a population of more than 22 million, making it one of the most populous urban areas in the world.

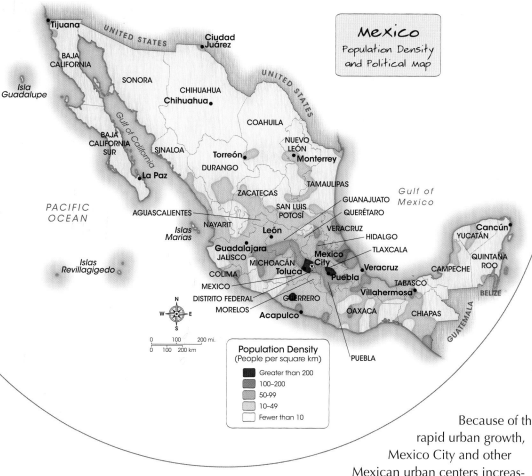

Mexico
Population Density
and Political Map

Gulf of Mexico

PACIFIC OCEAN

Population Density
(People per square km)

■	Greater than 200
▓	100–200
▒	50-99
░	10–49
□	Fewer than 10

Most Populous Cities

City	Population in millions
Mexico City	22
Guadalajara	4.7
Monterrey	3.6
Puebla	2.6
Tijuana	1.5
León	1.2
Toluca	1.2
Ciudad Juárez	1.1
Torreón	1.1

Because of this rapid urban growth, Mexico City and other Mexican urban centers increasingly suffered from the ills of overcrowding. So in the early 1980s, the government began to encourage businesses located in the downtown areas to relocate to the less crowded suburbs. As a result, the suburbs themselves grew rapidly. In the case of Mexico City, the suburbs combined with the inner city to form one giant metropolitan area.

The types of housing in Mexico's cities generally reflect the incomes of families that dwell in them. Teens from moderate- or low-income families live in

Homes of middle- and upper-income families are often painted in bright colors.

modest apartments or townhouses having a few small rooms. In these dwellings, siblings often share bedrooms. In contrast, wealthier families can afford larger apartments or townhouses with more rooms. Children in these families usually have their own bedrooms. Not surprisingly, the city dwellings of well-to-do families are also more elaborately furnished than those of lower-income families.

The Effects of Urban Poverty

These differences in size and degree of luxury in urban housing in Mexico's cities reflect a larger difference among the nation's economic classes. Mexico has the 13th strongest economy in the world. Yet the balance of wealth is very uneven—the poor are usually very poor and the wealthy are usually extremely wealthy.

Large numbers of people in Mexico City's metro area, as well as in other Mexican cities, fall into the low-income group. Some in this group live in small dwellings in slums on the outskirts of the cities. Often these humble homes—constructed of wooden planks, cinder blocks, or thin sheet metal—have little or no plumbing and heating facilities.

In city slums, sheet metal often forms the roofs of cinder-block homes.

Economically Uneven

In 2005, Mexico's gross domestic product was over the trillion-dollar mark, making it the 13th strongest economy in the world. Yet wealthy people make up only a small proportion of the country's population. A far larger proportion lives in poverty. Thus there is an uneven distribution of wealth in the country. The top 20 percent of earners account for 55 percent of the country's income. Meanwhile, the bottom 20 percent claim just 3 percent of the money.

Police Brutality

One of the major problems impoverished urban youth face is abuse and excessive force by police officers. In May 2004, for instance, demonstrators were tortured and abused by members of several police units. In another incident a year later, police officers killed three university students during an arrest that turned out to be a case of mistaken identity. Other reported violence includes unlawful killings by security forces, kidnappings by police, torture to force confessions, poor prison conditions, violence against women, and discrimination against indigenous people.

The use of torture as a means of control by the police violates international treaties. However, laws related to the treaties have not been enforced. While the government has investigated several incidences of security forces' involvement in criminal acts, officers were rarely punished for violence.

Human-rights activists have organized a number of protests in cities and along the Mexico–United States border in an attempt to prevent further attacks on Mexican citizens.

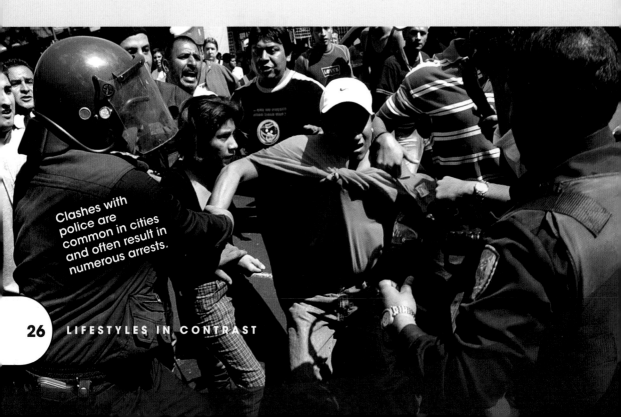

Clashes with police are common in cities and often result in numerous arrests.

A new low-cost housing subdivision north of Mexico City offers computer and high-speed Internet connections as standard features.

They are often poorly insulated, so they can get quite cold in the wintertime. Some parts of the urban slums have unpaved roads and open sewers. Mexicans call the worst of these slums the *ciudades perdidas*, or "lost cities."

In the 1940s, hundreds of thousands of the inhabitants of Mexico City lived in such lost cities. Hoping to reduce the problem, the government developed several large urban public housing projects. The most ambitious of these projects was the Nonoalco-Tlatelolco housing complex. It featured small but sturdy and comfortable living spaces for about 12,000 families. However, this attempt to provide affordable housing for the urban poor was not long-lasting. The public projects did not provide enough housing units to accommodate the huge numbers of rural Mexicans who migrated into Mexico City and other cities in the past 20 years.

ciudades perdidas
syew-DAH-days pair-DEE-dahs

Typical Schedule of an Urban Teen

5:15 A.M.	Rise and eat breakfast
8 A.M.	Attend four hours of school
12:30 P.M.	Work on homework
2 P.M.	Eat lunch
4 P.M.	Go to work, if the teen has a job
6 P.M.	Spend time with friends; perhaps have a light snack
9 or 10 P.M.	Enjoy the evening meal at home with family

Because some students go to school in the morning, and others go in the afternoon, parts of this schedule may be reversed. For example, teens who attend school in the afternoon would do homework or work at their jobs in the morning.

Life in the Countryside

The teens in Mexico's rural areas obviously do not have to deal with the kind of overcrowding that some of their urban counterparts do. Yet people in the countryside often face difficulties as challenging as those in the cities. Poverty is widespread in many rural sections of Mexico, for instance. And most rural residents work long hours filled with intensive physical labor on farms or fishing boats.

The rural sectors where teens live and sometimes work include farmlands that grow high-yield crops such as wheat, corn, and soybeans;

Fishers often live in small homes along the ocean.

Health Risks

Mexicans in poverty often suffer from health problems because of poor living conditions and limited access to health insurance and care. Health problems can be caused by a lack of housing, poor hygiene, unhealthful water storage practices, and little or no understanding of health risks.

Every year, unsafe sewage disposal is responsible for 3.2 million premature deaths. Another estimated 160,000 people live with HIV or AIDS. Those who live in rural areas often lack access to testing for, and prevention information about, HIV and AIDS.

In communities without running water, people must carry water from an area well.

Groceries are often bought at outdoor markets, which offer a variety of fresh produce.

low-density rain forests, in which people tend fruit trees, cut timber, and harvest plants to make various medicines; and coastal regions dotted with fishing villages. These rural areas are essential to Mexico's economic prosperity and the survival of all of its people. Farming, fishing, and other rural industries produce many important staples of everyday life, as well as a large portion of the country's exports.

Food & Drink

Among the many items produced in Mexico's rural regions, the most plentiful and important are various kinds of food and drink. With the exception of a few products imported from other nations, almost everything that Mexicans eat and drink is grown or made in the country. And they have become used to certain kinds of distinctive foods for their breakfasts, lunches, and dinners.

For breakfast, for example, many Mexicans, especially those who must leave for work early in the morning, are used to eating light. They typically have a cup or two of home-brewed coffee and a spiced tortilla or chunk of sweet bread. Alternatives for light eaters include orange juice with a slice of cantaloupe or one or two eggs. Those who prefer a larger breakfast often sit down to a meal of sweet breads, tortillas,

molletes
mo-YAY-tays

comida
co-MEE-dah

green and red salsas, fried eggs, or *molletes*, which are toasted bread rolls swathed in refried beans, cheese, and salsa.

At lunchtime, many working people in Mexico cannot make it home to eat with their families, but those who can usually do so. *Comida*, or lunch, is often the largest, most varied, and most satisfying meal of the day. The contents of that meal differ from one region of the country to another and from family to family. But one thing about comida is the same everywhere. It traditionally features up to six courses of delicious foods seasoned with savory sauces

A typical midday meal might include soup, pasta or rice, and a meat dish accompanied by vegetables, beans,

Food stands offer complete meals to lunchtime customers.

Churros, strips of deep-fried pastries sprinkled with sugar, are a popular treat. They are sold by vendors on city streets.

tortillas, and a thick salsa. Sometimes, especially for middle-income urban Mexicans, the meal is topped off with a tropical fruit salad.

After school or work and before supper, many teens enjoy an evening snack, which usually consists of coffee, milk, and perhaps leftovers from a previous comida. *Cena*, or supper, is eaten in the evening. Though often in itself a substantial meal, it is usually much lighter than lunch. Still the foods eaten at cena are most often similar to those at lunch—pasta, beans, meat, vegetables, and fruit.

For drinks, teens sip fruity beverages called *aguas frescas*. They can choose from flavors like *tamarindo*, made

cena
SAY-nah or
SEN-nah

aguas frescas
AW-gwa FRAY-cahs
tamarindo
tah-mah-REEN-doh

Aguas frescas are sold at roadside stands as well as in stores and restaurants.

from tamarind; *horchata*, from rice; or Jamaica, from hibiscus flowers. Favorite hot drinks include coffee and hot chocolate, usually flavored with fresh cinnamon.

Depending on the area or neighborhood, any and all of these popular drinks may be viewed as preferable to water. "Don't drink the water," a common phrase spoken by many visitors to Mexico, is also well-known to residents. Though the tap water in many areas is perfectly fine, in others it is frequently polluted and can cause stomach cramps. This is especially true in Mexico City, where water must be specially treated with filters and chemicals before drinking.

For residents and tourists who insist on drinking water, bottled water is sold just about everywhere.

horchata
or-CHAH-tah

Fast Food

In addition to enjoying traditional foods, Mexicans also consume a fair amount of fast food, like people in many other countries. Large American fast-food chains that have opened restaurants in Mexico include McDonald's, Burger King, Wendy's, Carl's Jr., Dairy Queen, Applebee's, Chili's, Bennigan's, Subway, Pizza Hut, Denny's, and Tony Roma's.

33

Teens often help care for younger brothers and sisters. The siblings form close relationships.

3

The Core of Society

FAMILY LIES AT THE CORE OF MEXICAN SOCIETY. SOME FAMILIES ARE NUCLEAR—consisting of a father, mother, and children. But at least as many are extended, with grandparents, aunts, uncles, cousins, and sometimes in-laws living in the same house. It is not uncommon to see 20 or more family members from several generations living under the same roof.

In such cases, the young people of the family are expected to show respect to their elders. In Mexican culture, the older genera-tions—parents, grandparents, and great-grandparents—are seen as sources of wisdom, experience, and authority.

Mexican society places just as much importance on young people as it does on their elders, although in a different way.

Who Is In Charge?

According to Mexican tradition, fathers are the moneymakers of families and therefore the heads of households. However, in many cases, mothers or other female family members run the household and look after the family on a daily basis. Some people believe that these resourceful women draw inspiration and strength from the Virgin of Guadalupe, the country's patron saint. According to Roman Catholic tradition, the Virgin Mary appeared to a man named Juan Diego on December 9, 1531, and spoke these words to him: "I am the mother of all of you who dwell in this land." In the centuries since, Mexicans look to the Virgin Mary for strength and protection.

Children: A Source of Pride

No matter how many people there are in a Mexican family, young children are generally seen as great sources of pride to everyone. And it is common for parents, grandparents, and other relatives to show off their children at

Common Names in Mexico

Boys	Girls
Antonio	Alicia
Carlos	Ana
Emilio	Angelica
Enrique	Beatriz
Hector	Juanita
Javier	Manuela
Juan	Maria
Rafael	Mia
Santiago	Rosa
Víctor	Rosario

It is common for families to work together. A Zapotec Indian family produced handmade rugs together for six generations.

attention and praise. In many families, teenagers receive as much time, consideration, and care from their parents and other family elders as the younger children do.

Partly because children are a source of pride in Mexican families, parents and older relatives often like to have young people continue living at home for as long as possible. Thus, it is fairly common for young adults to remain in their parents' houses until they are married. Even as young adults, the family's children continue to receive attention, praise, and privileges. In fact, in economically stable families where children do not have to work, young people are often not required to do any household chores either.

social gatherings. For such occasions, caring relatives lovingly shower attention on the little ones, making sure their clothes are on just right and their hair and nails are well-groomed.

But the youngest children are not always the only ones singled out for

What Time Is Curfew?

Although Mexican parents and grandparents often pamper their children, they also set rules and limits and impose discipline when necessary. For instance, it is common for parents to set curfews for their offspring. Mexico has no national curfew, but most families expect their children to be home by a certain hour. More often than not, young people stick to their curfews closely, either out of respect for their elders or fear of punishment. A common curfew time for teenagers is 10:30 P.M.

When Families Must Split Up

In some Mexican families, however, the children do have to find jobs. Poorer families, especially those living in areas where jobs are scarce, frequently find it difficult to make ends meet—there is not enough money to house, clothe, and feed everyone in the family.

One way that some families handle this problem is to send one or more of the children away. Younger children usually go to neighboring towns to live with

Nine-year-old Javier Robles works to contribute to his family's monthly income of 1,000 pesos (U.S.$92).

relatives who have smaller families and are more economically secure. One reason children are singled out is that they have fewer important responsibilities at home. They may also be seen as being more flexible and more able to adapt to new situations than older people.

In contrast, some older children are encouraged to leave home to find work in neighboring towns or cities. Because poorer families cannot afford to own cars, these young people cannot

travel from home to work and back again each day. So they must find places to live in the areas in which they work. Sometimes they live with relatives or friends; other times, they rent rooms in local homes. When possible, these young workers send any extra money they make back to their families.

Teens are not the only ones who leave their hometowns in search of work. Sometimes older children, in their 20s, and even grandparents, in their 50s

Leaving the Country

Many teens in Mexico must face the critical and difficult decision of whether to immigrate to the United States for work. The United States often offers more and better jobs, allowing the young workers to provide more financial support for their families. The young people regret having to leave their families, but this separation has become an expected part of life in Mexico.

The immigrants can still face a number of problems in the United States. More than half of the nearly 10 million Mexican immigrants in the United States live in poverty, while one-third are uninsured. Many remain uneducated and are unable to perform more than unskilled labor.

Juan, a 19-year-old who moved to the United States with his family, said: *"My family lives in a trailer house. We're seven brothers and three sisters. … When the night comes we all sleep wherever. Sleep on the floor, kitchen, wherever. … You see, my dad is working. Right now he's got this job that only pays around one-sixty [U.S.$160] a week … What is one-sixty a week for a big family like us? … Sometimes we don't even have food on the table."*

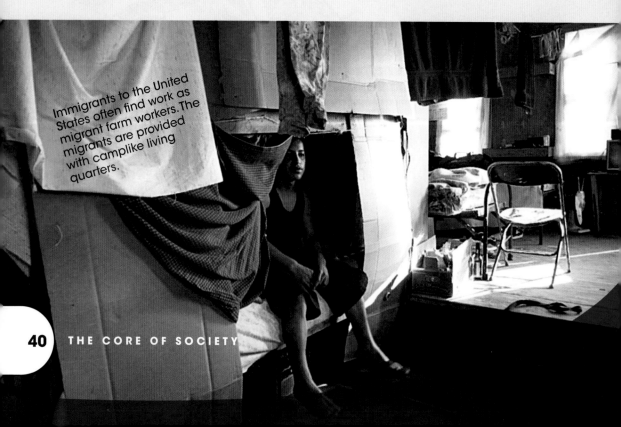

Immigrants to the United States often find work as migrant farm workers. The migrants are provided with camplike living quarters.

Families often gather on Día de los Muertos (Day of the Dead).

or 60s, must leave the extended family to find work.

When there are not enough jobs in neighboring towns and cities, these workers are forced to travel to more distant communities. Some even go so far as to migrate to the United States, where jobs are usually more plentiful. Once again, a large portion of money these family members make is sent home to help the main family.

Some parents in large families also feel they need to find work in places far from home. Parents who are gone for extended periods leave their younger children in the care of grandparents and other relatives. In some cases, these older caretakers are physically unable to perform all the daily chores. It is not unusual for teenagers and even preteens to end up doing much of the cleaning, cooking, shopping, and other daily tasks.

Even when Mexican families are split by distance, family members recognize that they are still connected by strong ties. They stay in touch with one another on a regular basis. And they try to attend family get-togethers held to celebrate birthdays, weddings, public holidays, religious holidays, and funerals.

Friends & Dating

Family ties are not the only strong connections that bind people in Mexican society. Friendships are many, and they tend to form early in life. By the time he or she is a teenager, a young man or woman usually has numerous friends with whom to share leisure activities such as playing sports, going to the movies, and dating. Among these friends are typically a few very close ones. A close friend is referred to as *amigo*; this term translates as "friend." As a rule, though, only close friends are addressed that way.

amigo
ah-MEE-go

A certain degree of familiarity, or comfort level, usually exists within one's circle of close friends in Mexican society. That comfort level is maintained partly through the use of nicknames that might be viewed as insults

My "Twin Brother"

In Mexico, boys, male teens, and adult men tend to form strong relationships with a small group of other male friends. The word *cuate* is used by boys and young men throughout the country to refer to a close male friend, as well as to one's entire group of friends. Cuate derives from an old Aztec Indian word meaning "twin brother." Such close male friends usually spend much of their time together, sometimes just hanging out, other times sharing very personal, private information. Those boys and men who bond this way typically think of one another almost as family.

cuate
coo-AH-tay

Skateboarding is a popular pastime among friends in urban areas.

gordo
GOHR-doh

flaco
FLAH-coh

in many other cultures. For example, it is common for both young people and adults to call a good buddy *gordo*, meaning "fattie," or *flaco*, meaning "skinny." In addition to such descriptive terms, Mexican teens often make up special nicknames for their closest friends.

Teens in Mexico tend to form close friendships with others of the same gender. And while close friendships between boys and girls are rare, dating is commonplace, from the big cities to the rural areas. An average Mexican date consists of going out for dinner, dancing, or a movie. In past generations, almost all dating situations were expected to lead to marriage. However, in the past 20 years, social changes made Mexican society less strict in many ways; as a result, dating became more casual.

Gerardo Turrubiartes, a young man in the state of San Luis Potosí, wrote on his personal Web page that although it was common for his friends to have girlfriends, he was happy to be single: *"I don't have to spend my money on gifts or stuff like that. Sometimes I date girls from the school. And more or less in each date I spent 100 or 200 pesos (U.S.$9 or $18). That's why I don't date too often."*

Keeping in Touch

One way that both family members and friends stay in touch with one another in Mexico is through the use of cell phones. Though they are far more common in cities than in small towns and rural areas, cell phones are used regularly throughout the country. Despite being convenient, they do have certain drawbacks. Perhaps the biggest of these is that Mexico has only one major telephone company—Telcel—to provide service for the entire country. As a result, there is little or no competition, and the choices in cell-phone services offered by the company are limited. Most cell-phone customers in Mexico have prepaid or pay-as-you-go phones. This way, they have more control over the cost of their phones.

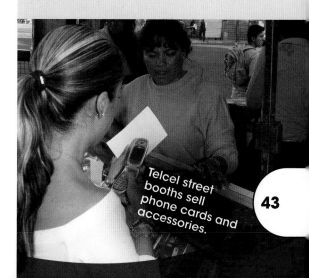

Telcel street booths sell phone cards and accessories.

Teens often participate in public celebrations, sometimes by performing traditional dances in parades.

4

Mexican Fiestas

MEXICANS OF ALL AGES AND WALKS OF LIFE ENJOY THE FESTIVITIES SURROUNDING BIRTHDAYS AND WEDDINGS. They also take part in a wide range of other celebrations over the course of the entire year. Some of these are religious in nature, others are cultural, and still others are connected to public holidays. In general, people refer to the parties held on such occasions as fiestas.

These celebrations are vital and significant parts of Mexican culture. The holidays offer people an opportunity to temporarily escape from their day-to-day duties and struggles. They can relax and enjoy themselves in the company of others.

Happy Birthday!

In Mexico, birthday parties are among the most common social gatherings and celebrations. Because most Mexicans are devoutly religious, they often make going to church or participating in other religious activities part of their birthday celebrations. When possible, a person associates his or her birthday with a day that honors one of the many Catholic saints. If one's birthday falls on the same day as that saint's day, which is often the case, there are two celebrations. The first, honoring the saint, is usually quiet and formal. It includes going to church and being blessed by a priest. The second celebration consists of a festive party held in the home of the birthday boy or girl.

Girls dress in elegant quinceañera gowns for their special day.

These parties are attended by family and friends, and often everyone in the neighborhood or village is invited to take part in the festivities. Typically, there are colorful decorations and lots of music and dancing. In addition, drinks and a wide variety of tasty homemade foods are served. Party games are also quite common. One of the most popular involves the traditional Mexican piñata. Most often, it consists of a large hollow animal filled with candy or other treats and suspended by a rope; the birthday boy or girl swings a stick or bat at the piñata, breaking it open and showering the room with goodies.

For girls, one birthday in particular, the *quinceaños*, or 15th birthday, is viewed as more important than the others. In honor of the occasion, families host a *quinceañera*, a coming-of-age party. In most Mexican families, the quinceañera is as important as a wedding celebration. This get-together is more than a party to note the passage of another year. It is also an acknowledgement that a girl is growing up and becoming an adult, something she has looked forward to for many years.

quinceaños
keen-see-AHN-nyos
quinceañera
keen-see-AHN-nyair-ah

The Traditional Birthday Song

The traditional Mexican birthday song is "Las Mañanitas." Its words translate into English as:

This is the song
that King David sang
to the pretty young girls.
We sing it here to you.

That the watchman on the corner
Would do me the favor
Of turning off his lantern
While my love passes.

OK now, Mr. Watchman,
I appreciate the favor:
Light you your lantern
Because my love has passed by.

Awake my fine one, awake,
Look, it has already dawned;
The birds are already singing,
The moon has already set.

The day that you were born,
All of the flowers were born;
At the baptismal font
The nightingales sang.

I would like to be a sunbeam
To enter through your window
And wish you good morning
Lying on your bed.

From the stars of the heavens
I would like to bring down two:
One to say hello to you
And the other to say goodbye.

Now it is already dawning
And the day has already given us light;
Rise up for the morning,
Look, it has already dawned.

47

The quinceañera attends Mass at the front of the church.

This celebration normally takes place on the first Saturday following the girl's birthday and begins with a thanksgiving Mass, a Catholic church service. Dressed in a white or light-colored dress, the young woman, also called the quinceañera, looks like a bride, wearing a headdress and carrying a bouquet. Following the service, friends and family enjoy a reception, complete with a meal, cake, and dancing.

The quinceañera dances her first dance, a waltz, with her father, but throughout the night, each of the men who attend will have a dance with her. Also during the reception, the girl's headpiece is replaced by a tiara, presented to her by a parent or godparent. It is a symbol that she is a princess before God. Toasts and a cake-cutting round out the festivities.

Traditional Quinceañera Gifts

Scepter—a symbol of the authority and responsibility that the young woman now has as an adult

Bracelet—a symbol of the unending circle of life

Earrings—a reminder to listen to God's word

Bible, cross, and rosary—symbols of her religious faith

bodas
BOH-dahs

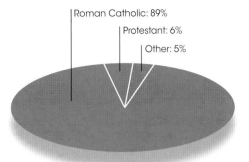

Religion in Mexico

Roman Catholic: 89%

Protestant: 6%

Other: 5%

Source: United States Central Intelligence Agency.
The World Factbook—Mexico.

Mexican Weddings

Another rite of passage for many young Mexicans is their *bodas*, or wedding. Wedding celebrations are viewed as important and powerful moments in the lives of the bride and groom, who are probably relatively young. The average age to marry in Mexico is 19.

Some 89 percent of Mexicans are devout Roman Catholics. Couples who are married almost always have a formal ceremony in a church before a priest. The commonly held belief among Mexicans is that marriage is a sacrament established by and honoring God.

Some Mexican brides choose to carry a fan, rather than a bouquet of flowers.

In addition to the traditional aspects of Catholic weddings everywhere, many Mexican couples add some extra colorful touches during the exchange of vows. One is the *arras*, a word that comes from the Latin term for marriage vows. A set of blessed coins are exchanged between the bride and groom to symbolize the security of their marriage. Another touch, the *lazo*, is a sort of necklace decorated with pearls, a cross, or fresh flowers. It symbolically links the bride and groom. A third touch many Mexicans add to their wedding ceremonies is a white veil called a *velo*, which the bride wears to symbolize her purity.

velo
VAY-loh

arras
AH-rras

lazo
LAH-zoh

Religious Celebrations

Like weddings, many of the holidays and celebrations that are observed in Mexican culture also stem from the Roman Catholic religion. Some of these include Navidad (Christmas), Pascua (Easter), and Día de la Virgen de Guadalupe (Day of the Virgin of Guadalupe). Each holiday features

Mexico City's Zocalo Square, an important city area, is dramatically lit for Christmas each year.

numerous traditional and popular customs. On December 24, for example, Mexicans celebrate the birth of Jesus Christ with cries of "*¡Feliz Navidad!*" meaning "Merry Christmas!"

The *posada* is another part of Mexico's Navidad traditions. Posadas are staged re-enactments of the biblical story about Joseph and Mary looking for a place to spend the night in Bethlehem before the birth of their son Jesus. Between December 16 and December 24, some families in Mexico invite neighbors over to their homes to re-create that famous event.

Also, four teens of the same height carry statues of Mary and Joseph riding donkeys. To be chosen as one of these re-enactors is considered an honor. Along with the posadas are Nativity scenes, which show baby Jesus lying in a manger surrounded by friendly people and animals. People set them up in town squares, in front of churches, on front lawns, and in other public places during the Christmas season.

On December 12, about two weeks

Feliz Navidad
fay-LEES nah-vee-DAHD

posada
poh-SAHD-ah

For the Three Kings

On January 6, Mexicans celebrate Día de los Reyes (Three Kings Day) to commemorate the arrival of the three wise men who, according to the Bible, visited and brought gifts to the baby Jesus. In Mexico people open most of their gifts on Día de los Reyes. In contrast, in many other Christian countries, gifts are given on Christmas Eve or Christmas Day.

A crown-shaped bread is often served on Día de los Reyes.

before Christmas, many Mexicans celebrate Día de la Virgen de Guadalupe. Though the Virgin of Guadalupe is acknowledged year-round throughout Mexico, on this particular day, many people journey to a shrine dedicated to her in Mexico City. Other people choose to celebrate this important religious holiday and fiesta at home, where they prepare a feast for family and friends.

Another important religious holiday in Mexico, Pascua, is the Christian celebration of Christ's resurrection following his crucifixion. Most Mexicans fulfill their religious duties and observe the traditional rituals of Semana Santa, or Easter week. But Pascua has also become the country's biggest holiday and party time. In fact, most Mexicans take the entire week off from work and other household duties to take part in the various festivities conducted by both families and communities. Teens usually have the whole week off from school as well. Deeply religious and solemn, as well as popular with the public, Pascua celebrations feature customs ranging from passion plays and feasts to games played by children of all ages.

Cultural & National Holidays

One of Mexico's more popular national holidays typically features scenes of teens sitting with their families on a soft blanket in the grass spread out over the grave of grandparents. In front of the headstone rests a picnic basket overflowing with freshly

Churches across Mexico honor Pascua (Easter) with outdoor celebrations.

baked breads. The sun set hours earlier, and candles glow brightly along the edges of the graveyard and in glass containers near each family. Yet the scene is not gloomy or morbid, as one might expect in a graveyard. Instead, people express their happiness as they remember their loved ones.

Public Holidays in Mexico

Año Nuevo (New Year's Day)—January 1
Día de la Constitución (Constitution Day)—February 5
Natalicio de Benito Juárez (Birthday of Benito Juárez)—March 21
Día del Trabajo (Labor Day)—May 1
Batalla de Puebla (Anniversary of the Battle of Puebla, or Cinco de Mayo)—May 5
Día de la Independencia (Independence Day)—September 16
Día de la Raza (Day of the Race)—October 12
Día de los Muertos (Day of the Dead)—November 2
Día de la Revolución (Revolution Day)—November 20
Día de la Virgen de Guadalupe (Day of the Virgin of Guadalupe)—December 12
Navidad (Christmas)—December 25

What Is an Ofrenda?

Día de los Muertos rituals have been followed for thousands of years by indigenous groups such as the Aztec, Maya, Nahua, P'urhépecha, and Totonac.

Ofrendas are altars, often built by families around the time of Día de los Muertos to celebrate the lives of loved ones. The ofrendas are often made from foods and drinks that were favorites of the deceased, or they're made from flowers, candles, and photos of the deceased. Mexicans feel that these objects help to relieve the somber atmosphere of death and allow families to fondly remember those who have passed on.

ofrendas
oh-FRAYN-das

This graveyard celebration is called Día de los Muertos, meaning "Day of the Dead." It is traditionally observed on November 2. Though it falls near other well-known worldwide holidays—such as Halloween, All Saints' Day, and All Souls' Day—and shares some similarities

with them, Día de los Muertos is a completely separate and unique holiday. Its customs come from a combination of ancient Indian mystical beliefs and lore and the teachings and customs of Roman Catholicism.

　　With its bright colors, laughing children, and food and drink, this native Mexican holiday might not seem like much more than a midnight picnic. But in fact, many of the events are connected to religious and spiritual ideas. Samples of the food and drink are "given" to the dead as symbolic offer-

Skeleton faces set off traditional clothing for Día de los Muertos celebrations.

ings—usually at every gravesite. Prayers are offered throughout the special night. Sometimes people even speak directly to the dead.

But beyond its serious side, Mexicans see and embrace elements of humor in Día de los Muertos. For example, one major symbol of the holiday is the *calavera*—a skull or skeleton. People construct dioramas featuring skeletons, paint their faces to look like skulls, and wear skeleton suits in parades. Instead of viewing these images of the dead as spooky and scary, most Mexicans make light of them; that way, the celebration becomes more about life than death.

Mexicans celebrate two other important national holidays: Día de la Independencia (Independence Day) and Batalla de Puebla, or Cinco de Mayo. Día de la Independencia honors

calavera
cah-lah-VAY-rah

Mexican flags become popular sales items for street vendors around Día de la Independencia.

September 16, 1810, the day when the Mexicans began their long war of independence against the Spanish. (Mexico finally gained full independence in August 1821.) Batalla de Puebla, on the other hand, celebrates a hard-won battle between a small Mexican army and a larger French army.

Batalla de Puebla is often mistaken for Mexican Independence Day in other countries, where people do not know the history behind the two national holidays. But Mexicans are well aware of the difference. And on both of these holidays, they stage elaborate festivities. Fireworks colored red, white, and green, like the Mexican flag, burst through the skies on both days, signifying all that the nation and its people have accomplished.

The Battle of Puebla

Cinco de Mayo (May 5) celebrates the Mexican victory in the 1862 Battle of Puebla. After about 8,000 French troops landed on Mexico's eastern coast and began marching toward Mexico City, the Mexicans responded with courage and ingenuity. Greatly outnumbered by the enemy, the Mexicans sent a herd of cattle stampeding into the French ranks. This created a gap into which the Mexicans charged, and eventually the tide of battle turned in their favor.

By the time they reach their teens, many rural children have been working for several years.

5

A Hardworking People

THOSE WHO LIVE IN MEXICO'S URBAN AND RURAL AREAS WORK IN A WIDE VARIETY OF JOBS. In the cities, many people work in factories or shops. Many others are employed in service jobs such as banking, law enforcement, firefighting, teaching, cooking or waiting on tables in restaurants, cleaning, and driving taxis. In the countryside, people are engaged in all manner of growing, harvesting, and transporting crops, as well as in raising livestock, fishing, and logging.

Throughout most of Mexico, high-paying jobs—those of bank presidents, business executives, and college deans, for example—

Young workers are proud to earn their own money, which is oftentimes shared with the family.

are limited in number. And it is sometimes hard for average Mexicans to find jobs that pay well enough to support a large family. Many people end up working for minimum wage, which in Mexico City is equivalent to about U.S.$4 per day. As a result, the majority of Mexican families cannot rely on a single income. Typically, both the husband and wife work, and in many cases, some children or extended family members work, too, with everyone contributing to the combined family home.

In families in which one or more of the children must work, their jobs are usually part time. This is because most Mexican parents do not want their children to work full time. The general feeling is that holding down a full-time job might jeopardize the quality of a child's education. Many parents view schooling as more important for teens than earning extra money.

Even in households where teens have jobs, the parents expect them to maintain good grades in school. Except in the very poorest of families, the parents are likely to force their sons or daughters to quit their jobs if the work interferes with their schooling. Many Mexican parents have been known to take two or three extra jobs themselves in order to allow their children to concentrate solely on their education.

After Graduation

However, even when young people in Mexico do devote all their energies to schoolwork, there is no guarantee that they will find a high-paying job right after they graduate. Some young Mexicans make it through secondary school and preparatory school and get good grades all along the way. They then go on to college and manage to graduate, sometimes with honors. Having acquired the knowledge and skills to enter a chosen profession, they are eager to find a good job and make their mark in the world. But many young Mexican men and women in this position are disappointed to find that no well-paying jobs in their field are available.

One ray of hope for young people in this situation is that in the past two decades Mexico has witnessed considerable growth in various high-tech industries, such as computers and telecommunications. Many college graduates manage to find satisfactory work in these areas. However, the number of jobs open in such specialized industries remains smaller than the number of college graduates looking for such openings. So many of Mexico's best-educated young people end up taking jobs outside of their chosen fields. Some decide to enter the teaching profession, which requires a college degree.

For those who don't attend college, employment opportunities vary a great deal, depending on the time, place, and the needs of local job markets. When available, this work

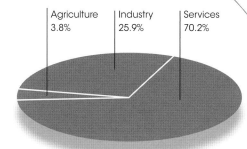

Division of Labor

| Agriculture 3.8% | Industry 25.9% | Services 70.2% |

Source: United States Central Intelligence Agency.
The World Factbook—Mexico.

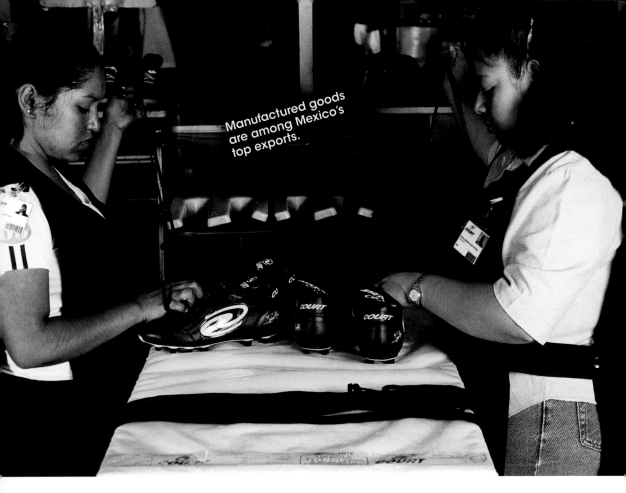

Manufactured goods are among Mexico's top exports.

includes trade jobs, such as electrician, plumber, and carpenter; factory work on assembly lines; clerking in retail stores; restaurant jobs; driving trucks, taxis, or limousines; and, the lowest-paying jobs of all, manual labor. Some of the young people who take these jobs find that they must, at least for a while, continue to live with their parents in order to make ends meet.

Not surprisingly, the majority of jobs in Mexico's rural areas are in agriculture. They include raising crops of beans, corn, wheat, soybeans, cotton, coffee, rice, tomatoes, and various fruits and vegetables. Some of the workers drive tractors and operate other machinery. Others store or process the foodstuffs or transport them to markets. In addition, many rural workers are involved in raising beef and dairy cattle, pigs, and chickens and other poultry.

These jobs usually require long hours. In the many small agricultural

Mexico
Land Use Map

N
W—E
S

0   100   200 mi.
0 100 200 km

Tijuana
UNITED STATES
Ciudad
Juárez
UNITED STATES

Isla
Guadalupe

PACIFIC
OCEAN

Torreón
Monterrey

Gulf of
Mexico

Cancún

Islas
Marías

León

Islas
Revillagigedo

Guadalajara

Mexico
City
Toluca
Puebla

Veracruz

BELIZE

GUATEMALA

Acapulco

Land Use
- Cropland
- Fruits and vegetables
- Forests
- Livestock
- Manufacturing
- Nonagricultural land

Underemployment

Even with a fairly low unemployment rate of 3.6 percent, Mexico suffers greatly from underemployment. People are considered underemployed when they have jobs but cannot afford life's necessities or support their families. Using this definition, it is estimated that the Mexican underemployment rate is 25 percent.

Workers at a coffee farm raked beans as they dried in the sun. The farm was flooded after a hurricane struck in 2005.

communities scattered across Mexico, the average workday starts before the sun rises and ends well after sundown. Almost all of these agricultural jobs also demand a certain degree of manual labor.

Some of that labor is done by teens. Many younger members of farm families help out for several hours in the morning and attend school in the afternoon, or vice versa. Typical chores include harvesting corn, coffee beans, and other crops; feeding cows, pigs, donkeys, and other farm animals; collecting eggs laid by chickens; cleaning out barns and chicken coops; and mending fences.

Working Women

Traditionally in Mexico, men were the providers and women took care of the household chores and the children. But in the past few decades, women have claimed both the home and the professional world as their workplaces. More and more women are not only completing primary and secondary school, but also going on to college and starting professional careers that previously only men pursued. Part of the reason for this shift is that in Mexico's struggling economy, families simply cannot survive on a single income. Women who may not have reached a high level of education still often work outside the home at difficult and physically strenuous jobs. They sometimes work 10- to 12-hour shifts before returning home to complete the household chores.

The Penoles Corporation employs women in its zinc- and lead- extraction operations.

The military consists of an army, air force, and navy.

Military Service

In Mexico, when a young man turns 18, he is required to sign up for the military and to serve for a minimum of 12 months. This law is designed mainly to ensure that Mexico has trained soldiers in case of an unexpected emergency. However, teens from middle- and upper-income classes rarely serve their time. In order to avoid the requirement, they often get physical deferments, which are easily obtained.

Women, too, serve in the military. Those who choose to enlist in the military face some restrictions. They are not allowed in combat, for example. Their service is limited to areas such as administration and medical care.

Neither the recruits nor their families normally worry that the young people will be killed or wounded in a foreign war or during an invasion of the country. Mexico has not taken part in any international war or other conflict in several decades, and it is unlikely to do so in the near future.

Mexicans are confident that none of their neighbors in North America will attack them, and they know that if forces from another part of the world tried to invade Mexico, the United States and other neighboring countries would immediately intervene. According to agreements signed by all of the nations of North America in the 1960s and 1970s, an attack on any of them is automatically viewed as an attack on all of them.

On the other hand, Mexican

Young People in Politics

A large proportion of young people in Mexico do not trust the government, particularly politicians and the police. They believe the government is unjust and corrupt. This has motivated a number of young Mexicans to establish equal-rights groups and to conduct demonstrations designed to bring attention to various causes close to their hearts.

Whether they are working toward creating more job opportunities or developing ties between Spanish-speaking Mexicans and indigenous peoples, many young Mexicans consistently show that they are concerned about the fate of their nation. Because voting is not required by law in Mexico, members of teen political groups often meet with their peers to discuss coming elections, in hopes of persuading them to vote for certain causes.

Young people often protest on issues related to education.

67

military recruits are well aware that they might see action and risk their lives in domestic disputes—those within Mexico's borders. Since the early 1990s, the country has experienced a number of social and political upheavals that required the intervention of the military. For instance, the military has contributed to efforts to end drug trafficking in the country, and troops are regularly assigned to carry out drug seizures.

Illegal Work

In addition to the large number of standard, respectable jobs and professions that exist in Mexico, there are also some illegal moneymaking activities that a small but growing part of the population engages in. The chief examples are the illegal drug trade and prostitution. Among the main reasons that these activities thrive are a lack of good jobs and extensive poverty, which exist in both the cities and rural areas.

Young women who are unable to find respectable employment and cannot afford to feed themselves or their children are sometimes drawn into prostitution. Teen pregnancy and the need for money to raise a child may be another reason women turn to prostitution. In Mexico, 15 percent of births are to teens between the ages of 15 and 19.

Some of these babies are unwanted and end up becoming "street children" who live on the streets or in city parks, often without homes of their own to return to. The street children often obtain

food and clothing by begging. In 2003, experts estimated that as many as 1.9 million street children between the ages of 12 and 17 were living in Mexico City, but the government claimed that the number was fewer than 6,000.

The other major source of

Street children often rely on charity organizations for hot meals.

be involved in drug trafficking, the world of the drug trade is male-dominated. Throughout Latin America, including Mexico, and the Caribbean, more than 75 percent of youths who are arrested on drug charges are male. Many of those involved are young—commonly teens who have dropped out of school. Despite efforts by the Mexican government and international organizations to wipe out the drug trade in Mexico, it shows no signs of slowing down.

Crossing the Border

Poverty and lack of employment opportunities in Mexico also cause many Mexicans, including teens, to immigrate illegally to Mexico's northern neighbor, the United States, in search of work. Most who resort to this option realize that it is an uncertain and even dangerous one. They have heard from friends and from news reports that crossing the border in hot desert regions and trying to escape capture by U.S. authorities can be filled with danger, even death. Since the U.S. Border Patrol began keeping track in October 1998, more than 1,900 people have died trying to cross the border.

But many people feel that the risks involved are worth taking. They gamble that they will be able to find some kind of work in the United States; if so, it will allow them to survive and also to send money back home to their needy family members.

illegal activities in Mexico, the drug trade, affects neighboring countries, including the United States, as much as Mexico itself. Cocaine and marijuana are the most common illegal drugs sold and used in Mexico. While people of both genders may

Crossing Coyotes

People who lead immigrants over the Mexico–United States border are called coyotes. Teens are often recruited for this job because immigration officials are more likely to let minors go if they're caught. The young coyotes often get involved because their families run smuggling businesses or they need the money.

Jose Luis, an 18-year-old ex-coyote, said that he got U.S.$450 per migrant he led over the border and another U.S.$300 to drive them to New Mexico. It was an easy job that paid better than his job at a fast-food restaurant. He said:

"I was working at McDonald's, not making very much, and I saw how much money my friends were making. It was so simple, so easy."

Teens who have been caught trying to cross the border wait for relatives to come to take them back to Mexico.

Leaving Mexico to find work in the United States is especially common among those who live in towns on the border between the two nations. But hopeful migrants come from cities and small towns all across Mexico. Often groups of Mexicans will pool their resources to find and pay someone who will drive them to the border. They also expect this person to smuggle them across without being captured by U.S. border guards. Immigrants who can't pay will often go it alone, even though it makes the trip riskier.

A metal and chain-link fence was built on the Tijuana–San Diego border in 2004, and President George W.

Bush signed a bill in 2006 authorizing U.S.$1.2 billion for strengthening border points. However, the projected number of immigrants has not decreased, and the average price for smuggling went up from U.S.$300 in 1994 to U.S.$2,500 in 2006. Experts say that barriers will make crossing more difficult and dangerous, but people will still take the risk.

Mexico
Topographical
Map

Tijuana
Laguna
Salada
Mexicali
UNITED STATES
Ciudad
Juárez

Existing border fence
Proposed border fence

Isla
Guadalupe

UNITED STATES

Conchos
River

Sierra Madre Occidental

Yaqui River

Fuerte R.

Bolsón de
Mapimí

Gulf of California

Baja California

Torreón

Sierra Madre Oriental

Rio Bravo del Norte

Central
Plateau

PACIFIC
OCEAN

Islas
Marías

Rio Grande
de Santiago

León

Guadalajara

Valley of
Anáhuac

Mexico
City

Pico de
Orizaba

Pánuco R.

Gulf of
Mexico

Cancún

Yucatán
Peninsula

Isla
Cozumel

Veracruz

Usumacinta
River

BELIZE

Islas
Revillagigedo

Sierra Madre del Sur

Balsas River

Acapulco

Grijalva
River

Isthmus of
Tehuantepec

Gulf of
Tehuantepec

GUATEMALA

N W E S

0 100 200 mi.
0 100 200 km

71

Often leisure time is spent hanging out with friends.

6

From Soap Operas to Soccer

PERHAPS BECAUSE THEY WORK SO HARD, MEXICANS WELCOME OPPORTUNITIES TO RELAX. Leisure time is enjoyed by people of all ages, and teens can escape their school work or daily labor in a number of ways. Sometimes they stay home and watch television, listen to music, or just hang out.

Other times, they go out to see movies, go to concerts, or cheer for their favorite sports teams.

Although teens in Mexico make time for their close friends, most free time is spent with family members. Consequently, spending time at home is always a great way to unwind.

Former Mexican soap stars form the singing group RBD. The group is incredibly popular in Latin American countries, such as Columbia and Brazil.

Escaping Through TV & Film

During those leisure hours that Mexicans choose to watch TV, many are captivated by programs called *telenovelas*. These are similar to the soap operas, or "soaps," that are widely popular in the United States and other English-speaking countries. However, the telenovelas contain considerably more violence and sex than their foreign counterparts. Though these shows appeal primarily to adults, a fair number of teens also tune in.

One soap was particularly popular with teens. *Rebelde* featured the life of preppy teens at a Mexican private school. The show ran from October 2004 to June

telenovelas
tay-lay-NOH-vay-las

2006, but the actors' popularity has raged on. Six of the show's attractive stars make up the pop singing group RBD— winner of three 2006 Billboard Latin Music Awards. In March 2006, the group opened a U.S. tour at the Los Angeles Coliseum. The concert set an attendance record by filling the stands with 60,000 fans.

In addition to the popular tele- novelas, the nine broadcast channels offered in Mexico show comedies, reality television, professional wres- tling, sports, and news programs. There are also many cable channels, which are usually available in all cities. They include still more sports broadcasts, plus shopping shows, cooking shows, game shows, and international news channels such as CNN and BBC News.

When Mexicans seek entertain- ment outside of the house, one of the more popular destinations is the cinema, or movies. In fact, going to the cinema is a weekly event in many Mexican families, especially for teens.

Typically groups of young people sit in a darkened theater holding plastic bags filled with candy made at home by their mothers. They avidly watch films with all types of themes and subjects—from adventure and action to love stories, horror flicks, and slapstick comedies. For most, the cinema offers a welcome relief from the everyday pressures of schoolwork or jobs.

Mexican Cinema

In the early 21st century, both Mexican films and Mexican film stars have become increasingly popular in other countries. For example, in 2004 a Mexican movie titled *Y Tu Mama Tambien (And Your Mother, Too)* received favorable reviews when shown in the United States and several European countries. Directed by Alfonso Cuaron, who was born in Mexico City in 1961, the film follows the adventures of two teenage Mexican boys who learn a great deal about life while on a road trip. Most movies produced in Mexico, however, are seen only in that country. Most are low- budget dramas and comedies.

Alfonso Cuaron (right) also directed Harry Potter & the Prisoner of Azkaban, starring Daniel Radcliffe.

Mariachi music serves as inspiration for certain traditional dances.

Musical Diversity

Music is another popular diversion that fills many leisure hours in Mexico. Common sources of music include home entertainment centers, car stereos, boom boxes, portable CD players, concerts staged in parks, and bands playing in nightclubs and bars. One of the more popular styles of music in Mexico is folk music, such as the traditional *ranchera* played by mariachi bands and marimba music from southern Mexico.

Mariachi is a blend of native Mexican, Spanish, and African musical styles, and includes violins, trumpets, guitars, and an acoustic bass guitar. A

ranchera
rahn-CHAY-ra

singer usually joins the other musicians to perform in restaurants, on the streets, or during weddings.

Marimba is more often a solo or small ensemble performance, with the musicians playing an instrument also called the marimba. The marimba is made from pipes or gourds of differing sizes that produce a percussive sound similar to that of the xylophone when tapped with mallets.

Also widely popular in Mexico is contemporary international music, including pop, rock, and hip-hop, as well as Mexican and Caribbean Island blends. Rapper Snoop Dogg, from the United States, is a favorite among Mexican teens. Popular, too, are contemporary Mexican rock and hip-hop favorites like the rock band Café Tacuba and the rap duo Crooked Stilo.

Equally well-liked among young Mexicans is *reggaeton*, a new style of music brought to Mexico from Puerto Rico. Reggaeton consists of a distinctive hybrid of styles, blending hip-hop, Jamaican reggae, and dance.

reggaeton
ray-geh-tone

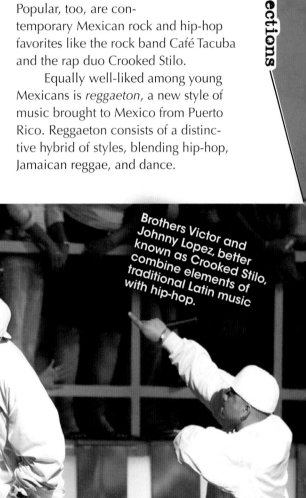

Brothers Victor and Johnny Lopez, better known as Crooked Stilo, combine elements of traditional Latin music with hip-hop.

When the national fútbol team wins a big game, celebrations often spill into the streets.

Sports & More

In addition to TV, movies, and music, millions of Mexicans of all ages enjoy sports. The most popular sport in the country—and the world, for that matter—is *fútbol* (soccer).

fútbol
foot-bole

The Mexican fútbol league has 18 teams, some of them named after states and cities, such as Chiapas, Toluca, Guadalajara, Veracruz, and Monterrey. These teams are so popular that even in the country's lower-income areas, most professional fútbol games sell out. And thousands of fútbol fans watch the matches on television.

The World's First Team Sport?

The tremendous popularity of fútbol in Mexico in some ways mirrors the popularity of ball games played by teams in the country's distant past. Historians think that one of the world's first team sports was invented in Mexico more than 3,500 years ago. The Indian people who dominated the region at that time, including the Aztecs and Olmecs, developed a ball game called *ollama* or *tlachtli*. It is uncertain how the game was played. But some surviving clues suggest that it centered on two teams of several players, a solid rubber ball made from the sap of the rubber tree, and a stone-walled ball court. The object may have been to use one's feet, knees, or hips to bounce the ball past the members of the opposing team and through a stone circle.

A sculpture from the Mayan Classic Period (c. 250–900) depicts a tlachtli player.

ollama
o-YA-ma

tlachtli
tla-chi-TLI

The most famous lucha libre stars often appear in movies, too..

Most games have a happy, friendly atmosphere, although now and then violence erupts at a game, especially when overzealous fans become upset with a player's performance or a referee's call.

In addition to watching fútbol, nearly every Mexican boy from every walk of life plays fútbol—whether with family, friends, or an organized league.

Girls and adults, too, participate in the sport in their free time, enjoying the exercise and the time spent with their friends.

Next to fútbol, one of the most popular sports-related pastimes in Mexico is watching *lucha libre*, or professional wrestling. Most

lucha libre
LOO-cha
LEE-bray

of the fans watch the matches on TV, though some attend in person. Most of the fans realize that the wrestlers are also actors and that the moves are staged and the outcomes of the matches are decided in advance. Yet the fans watch the matches anyway because they greatly enjoy the colorful and fast-paced spectacle. The more popular wrestlers also appear as characters in comic books, magazine series, and movies.

Reading & Other Arts

Another leisure pastime enjoyed by some Mexicans is reading books. The country's larger cities have libraries, where adults and teens can borrow books, ranging from old classics to current best sellers. During the summers, when young children and teens are out of school, many larger cities have reading and arts programs that provide activities at little or no cost. Some cities even offer "traveling libraries" as well as lessons in painting, music, theater, and other artistic fields.

For Mexican teens, comic books are the most popular reading material outside of school. The comics are available in Spanish, English, and even in various indigenous languages. The stories most often feature superheroes, popular wrestlers, and historical figures.

Online in Mexico

Still another leisure diversion for those Mexicans who can afford it is surfing the Internet. Only about 18 percent of families in Mexico have access to the Internet, but the number of Internet users is growing steadily.

Growth of the Internet in Mexico

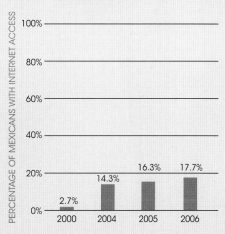

PERCENTAGE OF MEXICANS WITH INTERNET ACCESS

Year	Percentage
2000	2.7%
2004	14.3%
2005	16.3%
2006	17.7%

Source: Internet World Stats

81

Looking Ahead

THE LIFESTYLES OF MEXICO'S INHABITANTS, ESPECIALLY ITS TEENS, ARE RAPIDLY CHANGING. Contributing to cultural change are the continuing growth of cities, the creation of new industries and job opportunities, and the ongoing adoption of modern technologies. For instance, while many schools in poorer areas of the country are in a state of disrepair, more and more schools are using televisions, computers, and other electronic learning tools. These often help those who are falling behind to catch up with their classmates. Meanwhile, Mexico remains a country of diversity— culturally, ethnically, economically, and politically. A significant contrast exists between the lifestyles of city dwellers and people in the countryside; and ethnic and cultural differences between the indigenous Indian people and Mexicans of mixed heritage remain. Another major divide in the country—between rich and poor—continues as well. Because of poverty, increasing numbers of Mexicans, including many teens, migrate to the United States each year. It will be the task of those who stay behind to shape Mexico's future.

At a Glance

Official name: United Mexican States

Capital: Mexico City

People

Population: 107,449,525

Population by age group:
0-14 years: 30.6%
15-64 years: 63.6%
65 years and up: 5.8%

Life expectancy at birth: 75.41 years

Official language: Spanish

Other languages: English, and various indigenous languages, including Nahuatl and Maya

Religion:
Roman Catholic: 89%
Protestant: 6%
Other: 5%

Legal ages
Alcohol consumption: 18
Driver's permit (under
parent's supervision): 16
Driver's license: 18
Employment: no minimum
Marriage: 14 for females, 16 for males
Military service: 18
Voting: 18

Government

Type of government: Federal republic

Chief of state: President, elected by popular vote

Head of government: President, elected by popular vote

Lawmaking body: The Camara de Senadores (Senate) and Camara Federal de Diputados (Federal Chamber of Deputies) together make up the Congreso de la Union (National Congress)

Administrative divisions: 31 states and one federal district

Independence: September 16, 1810 (from Spain)

National symbols: The coat of arms on the national flag was inspired by an Aztec legend and features an eagle holding a snake in its talons. The colors of the flag symbolize the following: green symbolizes hope; white, purity or unity; red, religion or blood of national heroes.

Geography

Total Area: 789,020 square miles (1,972,550 square kilometers)

Climate: Varies between temperate and hot, humid

Highest point: Volcan Pico de Orizaba, 18,810 feet (5,700 meters)

Lowest point: Laguna Salada, 33 feet (10 m) below sea level

Major landforms: Sierra Madre Occidental, Sierra Madre Oriental, and Sierra Madre del Sur mountain ranges;

central plateau; two major valleys, the Bolsón de Mapimi and the Anáhuac

Major rivers: Rio Bravo, Pánuco, Grijalva, Usomacinta, Conchos

Economy

Currency: Mexican peso

Population below poverty line: 40%

Major resources and products: Petroleum, silver, copper, gold, lead, zinc, natural gas, timber

Major agricultural products: Corn, wheat, soybeans, rice, beans, cotton, coffee, fruit, tomatoes, beef, poultry, dairy products

Major exports: Manufactured goods, oil and oil products, silver, fruits, vegetables, coffee, cotton

Major imports: Metalworking machines, steel mill products, agricultural machinery, electrical equipment, car parts for assembly

Historical Timeline

Hernán Cortés arrives from Spain; less than two years later, Cortés and Indian allies conquer the ruling Aztecs

First battle in the war for independence from Spain, which is accomplished in 1821

The indigenous population of "New Spain" drops from 25 million to fewer than 3 million because of disease, religious persecution, and extreme poverty

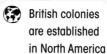 Inca civilization flourishes in South America

| 250 | c. 1000 | c. 1325 | 1519 | 1600s | 1800 | 1808 | 1810 |

Napoléon Bonaparte dethrones the Spanish king, provoking unrest throughout the empire

The Maya rise to prominence

 British colonies are established in North America

Aztecs found Tenochtitlán (Mexico City)

 Historical World Event

Constitution
establishes Mexico
as a republic with a
federal system

Mexico and the United States
are at war; in the resulting
Treaty of Guadalupe Hidalgo,
Mexico cedes present-day
Arizona, California, and
New Mexico and parts of
Colorado, Nevada, and
Utah to the United States

Guerrilla armies
led by Pancho
Villa and Emiliano
Zapata fight the
Mexican Revolution,
which ends with the
Constitution of 1917;
altered many times, it
remains in force today

Mexico nationalizes
foreign oil companies
operating in the
country; the nation's
economy benefits
from the need for oil
during World War II

 World War II

| 1824 | 1836 | 1846–1848 | 1854–1861 | 1910–1917 | 1929 | 1938 | 1939–1945 |

Benito Juárez and other
liberals overthrow Santa
Anna and initiate
reforms, including the
expanded Constitution
of 1857

Texas secedes
from Mexico

The U.S. stock market
crashes, and severe
worldwide economic
depression sets in

Historical Timeline

The North American Free Trade Agreement begins to phase out tariffs among the United States, Canada, and Mexico.

An enormous earthquake rocks Mexico City and much of the western portion of the country, killing thousands; furious citizens criticize the inadequate government response

 Terrorist attacks on the two World Trade Center towers in New York City and on the Pentagon in Washington, D.C., leave thousands dead

Conservative candidate Felipe Calderon is elected president in an extremely close race against leftist Andres Manuel Lopez Obrador

1968	1985	1989	1994	2000	2001	2005	2006

The Berlin Wall falls

Intensifying hostility between the authorities and drug gangs leads to the murders of six prison guards

Riot police repress student protests, killing more than 100 people in Mexico City; the summer Olympic Games are held there 10 days later

Vincente Fox is elected president, the first opposition candidate to beat the Institutional Revolutionary Party, which had governed since 1929

Glossary

curriculum	the courses of study offered at an educational institution
deferments	approved postponements of required military service
diorama	three-dimensional replication of a scene (often a miniature version)
discrimination	unfair treatment of a person or group, often because of race or religion
disparity	lack of equality or similarity
gross domestic product	the total value of all goods and services produced in a country
high-yield crops	crops that produce in abundance
hybrid	mixture
indigenous	native to a place
migrants	people who move to new areas or countries, often in search of work
persistent	existing for a long time; long-lasting
strenuous	difficult or challenging
urbanized	characterized by dense populations and other qualities of city life

Additional Resources

IN THE LIBRARY

Barlow, Genevieve, and William N. Stivers. *Stories from Mexico—Historias de Mexico*. New York: McGraw-Hill, 1995.

Coe, Michael D., and Rex Koontz. *Mexico: From the Olmecs to the Aztecs*. 5th ed. New York: Norton, 2002.

Hamilton, Janice. *Mexico in Pictures*. Minneapolis: Lerner, 2003.

Menard, Valerie. *The Latino Holiday Book*. New York: Marlow & Company, 2000.

Sheen, Barbara. *Foods of Mexico*. Detroit: Kidhaven Press, 2006.

Streiffert, Anna, ed. *Mexico*. Rev. ed. New York: DK Publishing, 2003.

ON THE WEB

For more information on this topic, use FactHound.
1. Go to *www.facthound.com*
2. Type in this book ID: 0756520649
3. Click on the *Fetch It* button.

Look for more Global Connections books.

Teens in Australia	*Teens in Kenya*
Teens in Brazil	*Teens in Russia*
Teens in China	*Teens in Saudi Arabia*
Teens in France	*Teens in Spain*
Teens in India	*Teens in Venezuela*
Teens in Israel	*Teens in Vietnam*
Teens in Japan	

Source Notes

Page 15, column 2, line 11: Laurie M. Scott. "Back to School Around the World." *The Christian Science Monitor*. 4 Sept. 2001. 23 June 2006. www.csmonitor.com/2001/0904/p13s1-lekt.html

Page 18, sidebar, line 13: "Mexico: Schools Without Leaks." *Worldbank.org*. 29 Aug. 2005. 18 May 2006. http://web.worldbank.org/WBSITE/EXTERNAL/COUNTRIES/LACEXT/MEXICOEXTN/0,,contentMDK:20627490~menuPK:50003484~pagePK:141137~piPK:141127~theSitePK:338397,00.html

Page 36, sidebar, line 15: "The Virgin of Guadalupe." *Casa Mexicana*. 23 June 2006. www.casamexicanafolkart.com/the_virgin_of_guadalupe.html

Page 40, column 2, line 9: "Teenage Diaries." *All Things Considered*. NPR. Washington, D.C. 5 July 1996. 13 Oct. 2006. www.radiodiaries.org/transcripts/TeenageDiaries/Juan.html

Page 43, line 32: Gerardo Turrubiartes. "Life in a State Shaped Like a Dog." Googolplex. 23 June 2006. http://googolplex.cuna.org/33408/cnote/story.html?doc_id=547

Page 47, sidebar, column 1, line 4: Dale Palfrey, trans. "Las Mañanitas." *Mexico Connect* 2006. 23 June 2006. www.mexconnect.com/mex_/travel/dpalfrey/dpmananitas.html

Page 70, sidebar, line 19: Barbara Ferry. "Teens Recall Smuggling for Thrills, Big Money." *The New Mexican*. 31 July 2006. 10 Oct. 2006. www.freenewmexican.com/news/47201.html

Pages 84–85, At a Glance: United States. Central Intelligence Agency. *The World Factbook—Mexico*. 17 Oct. 2006. 24 Oct. 2006. www.cia.gov/cia/publications/factbook/geos/mx.html

Select Bibliography

Augherton, Ann M. "Meet Fernando, Just One Street Kid in Mexico City." *Arlington Catholic Herald*. 20 Nov. 2003. 13 May 2006. www.catholicherald.com/articles/03articles/mexico1120.htm

Bensinger, Ken. "Mexico's Answer to Tight School Budgets: Teaching by TV." *The Christian Science Monitor*. 21 Oct. 2004. 24 Oct. 2006. www.latinamericanstudies.org/mexico/telesecundaria.htm

"Cellular Phone Services in Mexico." *Solutionsabroad.com*. 20 Dec. 2005. www.solutionsabroad.com/a_cellularphonesmexico.asp

Cobo, Leila. "Teen Soap 'Rebelde' Heats Up Latin Chart." *Monstersandcritics.com*. 13 Sept. 2005. 22 Jan. 2006. http://music.monstersandcritics.com/news/article_1047803.php?compage=80&comcount=211&comlimit=10

Ferriss, Susan. "Dateline: Mexico City: Mexicans Eat Up Satire TV Show." *The Atlanta Journal-Constitution*. 21 Sept. 2005. 22 Jan. 2006. www.ajc.com/search/content/auto/epaper/editions/wednesday/atlanta_world_3403eacd2004802000a3.html

Ferry, Barbara. "Teens Recall Smuggling for Thrills, Big Money." *The New Mexican*. 31 July 2006. 10 Oct. 2006. www.freenewmexican.com/news/47201.html

GenderStats: Database of Gender Statistics. "Summary Gender Profile." *Worldbank.org*. 18 May 2006. http://devdata.worldbank.org/genderstats/genderRpt.asp?rpt=profile&cty=MEX,Mexico&hm=home

Green, Greg. "Bicycling in the World's Largest City." *Planeta.com*. December 1994. 20 Jan. 2006. www.planeta.com/ecotravel/period/greg/mexbike.html

Hawley, Chris. "World Staying Tuned to Mexico Telenovelas." *Azcentral.com*. 23 Sept. 2004. 22 Jan. 2006. www.azcentral.com/specials/special42/articles/0923Telenovelas23.html

Linton, Malcolm. "Preventing Violence and Lowering Dropout Rate in Mexico City Schools." *UNICEF.org.* 9 Jan. 2005. 17 Jan. 2006. www.unicef.org/infobycountry/mexico_30660.html

Mavor, Guy. *Mexico, A Quick Guide to Customs and Etiquette.* Portland, Ore.: Graphic Arts Center Publishing Center, 2005

"Mexico." *Madre.org* 2004. 24 Jan. 2006. www.madre.org/countries/Mexico.html

"Mexico Internet Usage, Population and Telcommunications Reports." Internet World Stats. 16 Nov. 2006. www.internetworldstats.com/am/mx.htm

"Mexico: Schools Without Leaks." *Worldbank.org.* 29 Aug. 2005. 18 May 2006. http://web.worldbank.org/WBSITE/EXTERNAL/COUNTRIES/LACEXT/MEXICOEXTN/,,contentMDK:20627490~menuPK:50003484~pagePK:141137~piPK:141127~theSitePK:338397,00.html

Montes de Oca de Marshall, Assunta. "Mexican Traditions for Christmas." *Nacnet.org.* 14 May 2006. www.nacnet.org/assunta/nacimnto.htm

Palfrey, Dale, trans. "Las Mañanitas." *Mexico Connect* 2006. 23 June 2006. www.mexconnect.com/mex_/travel/dpalfrey/dpmananitas.html

Ross, John. *Mexico in Focus.* New York: Interlink Books, 2003

Scott, Laurie M. "Back to School Around the World." *The Christian Science Monitor.* 4 Sept. 2001. 23 June 2006. www.csmonitor.com/2001/0904/p13s1-lekt.html

"Teenage Diaries." *All Things Considered.* NPR. Washington, D.C. 5 July 1996. 13 Oct. 2006. www.radiodiaries.org/transcripts/TeenageDiaries/Juan.htm

"Timeline: Mexico." *BBC News.* 23 Oct. 2005. 31 Jan. 2006. http://news.bbc.co.uk/1/hi/world/americas/country_profiles/1210779.stm

Tompkins, Cynthia Margarita, and Kristen Sternberg. *Teen Life in Latin America and the Caribbean.* Westport, Conn.: Greenwood Press, 2004

Turrubiartes, Gerardo. "Life in a State Shaped Like a Dog." Googolplex. 23 June 2006. http://googolplex.cuna.org/33408/cnote/story.html?doc_id=547

"The Virgin of Guadalupe." *Casa Mexicana.* 23 June 2006. www.casamexicanafolkart.com/the_virgin_of_guadalupe.html

United States. Central Intelligence Agency. *The World Factbook—Mexico.* 17 Oct. 2006. 24 Oct. 2006. www.cia.gov/cia/publications/factbook/geos/mx.html

Index

About the Author
Brian Baumgart

Brian Baumgart has worked as a high school teacher, college instructor, and advertising copywriter. He writes fiction, nonfiction, and poetry, several pieces of which have been published in various magazines and journals. Brian holds a master's degree in creative writing from Minnesota State University, Mankato, and a bachelor's degree in English education from Winona State University.

About the Content Adviser
Miguel Angel Centeno, Ph.D.

A published author and editor, Miguel Angel Centeno serves as the director of the Princeton Institute for International and Regional Studies. He was also a Fulbright Scholar in Russia and Mexico. As our content adviser for Teens in Mexico, he offered unique insight and perspective to ensure an honest and balanced presentation of this engaging country.

Image Credits

Luc Novovitch/Alamy, cover; Alfredo Schaufelberger/BigStockPhoto, back cover (top), 90; Keith Levit/IndexOpen, back cover (bottom), 1 (middle right); Corel, 1 (left), 4, 7 (top), 85 (top); Kim Karpeles/Alamy, 1 (middle left), 72; Bob Rowan/ Progressive Image/Corbis, 1 (right), 8–9; Elisa Locci/Shutterstock, 2–3; Tomasz Otap/Shutterstock, 5; Patricia Marroquin/BigStockPhoto, 7 (middle); Jason Keith Heydorn/Shutterstock, 7 (bottom left); Elena Ray/Shutterstock, 7 (bottom right); Danita Delimont/Alamy, 10, 36–37, 41, 58; B&Y Photography/Alamy, 13; Keith Dannemiller/Corbis, 14, 62, 65; Spencer Grant/Art Directors, 15; Howard Sayer/ Art Directors, 16; Keith Dannemiller/D70s/Corbis, 17, 22, 27; AP Photo/Eduardo Verdugo, 19; Karen Huntt/Corbis, 20; Adalberto Rios Szalay/Sexto Sol/Photodisc Green/Getty Images, 24; Barry Lewis/Alamy, 25; AP Photo/Jose Luis Magana, 26, 57; trialart-info/Shutterstock, 28; AP Photo/Victor R. Caivano, 29; Bob Krist/ Corbis, 30; Danny Lehman/Corbis, 31; PCL/Alamy, 32; Steve Hamblin/Alamy, 33; Jeff Greenberg/Art Directors, 34; AP Photo/Marco Ugarte, 36 (bottom); AP Photo/David de la Paz, 38–39; AP Photos/Amy Sancetta, 40; Keith Dannemiller/ Alamy, 42, 43; Robert Frerck/Stone/Getty Images, 44; Robert Fried/Alamy, 46, 48; Photodisc, 47; ML Sinibaldi/Corbis, 49; Daniel Aguilar/Reuters/Corbis, 50–51; Andres Balcazar/iStockphoto, 52; Tristan da Cunha/Alamy, 53; Livia Corona/ Stone/Getty Images, 54–55; Henry Romero/Reuters/Corbis, 54 (bottom), 64; Elizabeth Ruiz/epa/Corbis, 56; Alamy, 60, 76; Liam White/Alamy, 66; AP/Wide World Photos, 67; Jack Kurtz/ZUMA/Corbis, 68–69; AP Photo/David Maung, 70–71; Alexander Tamargo/Getty Images, 74; Don Emmert/AFP/Getty Images, 75; Frank Micelotta/Getty Images, 77; Reuters/CORBIS, 78; Lauros/Giraudon/The Bridgeman Art Library, 79; Andrew Winning/Reuters/Corbis, 80; Shaul Schwarz/ Corbis, 82–83; Elisa Locci/BigStockPhoto, 84 (top); Bob O'Lary/BigStockPhoto, 84 (bottom); Carlos Sanchez Pereyra/Shutterstock, 85 (bottom).

border to border · teen to teen · border to border · teen to teen · border to border